FINANCI ACCOUNTING
PROJECTS

competency based

Using Microsoft® Office

ROGER A. GEE
San Diego Mesa College

South-Western College Publishing
Thomson Learning™

Australia • Canada • Mexico • Singapore • Spain • United Kingdom • United States

Financial Accounting Projects Using Microsoft® Office by Roger A. Gee
Acquisitions Editor: Sharon Oblinger
Marketing Manager: Larry Qualls
Production Editor: Heather Mann
Manufacturing Coordinator: Doug Wilke
Cover Design: Rick Moore

Printed in the United States of America
1 2 3 4 5 03 02 01 00

For more information contact South-Western College Publishing, 5101 Madison Road, Cincinnati, Ohio, 45227 or find us on the Internet at http://www.swcollege.com

For permission to use material from this text or product, contact us by
• telephone: 1-800-730-2214
• fax: 1-800-730-2215
• web: http://www.thomsonrights.com

ISBN: 0-324-02820-2

This book is printed on acid-free paper.

Message to Students

This workbook is designed to help you apply the accounting concepts discussed in your Financial Accounting textbook. Workbook projects cover the following themes:

- The accounting information system
- Analysis and interpretation of financial accounting information

While you are completing the projects, you will also learn a competency, which the Labor Secretary's Commission on Achieving the Necessary Skills [SCANS] found to be essential for success in the labor force. You will learn how to think while integrating spreadsheet, word processing, and presentation software. This computer skill is required in all good accounting, finance, marketing, and management jobs.

Each project has a section of required steps. Make sure that you complete the steps in order. Key verbs in the steps are underlined. Refer to the procedures in the Appendix. They are alphabetized by underlined verbs.

Project 13 requires you to participate in a group of three or more students. You will evaluate data that has no clear correct answer. You may be required to report the results of your work to the class using spreadsheet and word processing software. You may also demonstrate how stocks are monitored and how stock transactions are recorded.

Some of the projects are more complex than the material shown in your textbook. One reason is that you sometimes have to illustrate reports and presentations differently when integrating software packages. Another reason is that this workbook is meant to add value to what you learn from your textbook.

Take your time, and enjoy your projects!

Roger A. Gee
San Diego Mesa College

Thanks to the students in my Fall 1999 financial accounting classes.
I appreciate each error that they found and every suggestion
that they offered for improvement.

Contents

    Competencies:

- Integrate *Microsoft® Excel* and *Microsoft® Word* to create a report that evaluates the use of news articles, stock market prices, long-term trends, and financial statement analysis calculations for investing in stocks.
- Demonstrate how stocks are monitored and how stock transactions are recorded.

Project One

Three Major Business Activities

Competencies

- Use *Microsoft® Word* to create a report that explains financing, investing, and operating activities in a corporation and the types of decisions that they require.
- Identify examples of each major business activity that is shown on a statement of cash flows.

Financing Activities Data

Financing activities are methods Student's Name Corporation (your hypothetical company) uses to obtain financial resources from stockholders (investors) and creditors (lenders). The primary financial resource is cash. Financing decisions include:

- Sources and amounts of financing needed
- When and where financing is obtained
- What affect the financing will have on your corporation's profitability and survival

Investing Activities Data

Investing activities include the selection, disposal, replacement, and management of long-term resources that are used to develop, produce, and sell goods and services. Assume that the long-term resources used at Student's Name Corporation include land, buildings, equipment, and legal rights. Investing decisions include:

- What long-term resources are needed
- How much of each resource should be acquired
- When to acquire, sell, or replace resources

Operating Activities Data

Operating activities involve the use of resources to design, produce, distribute, and market goods and services. At Student's Name Corporation they include the day-to-day operations. Operating decisions concern:

- Research and development
- Marketing and selling
- Servicing

Required

A report generally has three elements: introduction, main body, and conclusion. In the introduction, tell the reader that you are going to discuss three major business activities—financing, investing, and operating. The introduction should be short—two or three sentences. The main body is used to present your facts in a logical manner. It is here that you explain financing, investing, and operating activities and give examples of the types of decisions made by management. The conclusion should be short—three or four sentences. You are allowed your opinion here. For example, you should indicate the most important business activities at Student's Name Corporation (your hypothetical company) and why.

Make sure that you complete the following steps in order. Refer to the procedures in the Appendix, which are alphabetized by underlined verb. Note the underlined verbs in the steps below.

---

1. <u>Open</u> *Word* and format a new document.
2. Enter a two-page report that explains financing, investing, and operating activities that are used in Student's Name Corporation (your hypothetical company). Also, describe the types of decisions that they require. The double-spaced report should be free of spelling and grammatical errors. Use information available in Chapter 1 of your textbook and the data on page 1.1 of this workbook. The title should be at the top of the first page. The title of the report is:

Three Major Business Activities
By
Student's Name

3. <u>Insert</u> footers into the *Word* document.
4. <u>Save</u> your project to a floppy disk.
5. <u>Print</u> the *Word* document.
6. Staple the Transmittal Sheet to the top of the report.
7. On the Transmittal Sheet, list two examples of each major business activity that is shown in any statement of cash flows from your textbook.

Project One Transmittal Sheet

Student Name: _____

Student Identification Number: _____

Class: _____

Date: _____

_____
_____
_____
_____
_____
_____
_____
_____
_____
_____
_____
_____
_____
_____
_____
_____
_____
_____
_____
_____
_____
_____

Notes:

Project Two

Two Accounting Equations

Competencies

- Use *Microsoft*® *PowerPoint* to create a presentation that defines two accounting equations and classifies major accounts used by a corporation.
- List the major accounts used by a corporation and identify the financial statement in which each appears.

Project Data

Slide 1. Title and sub-titles along with type sizes

<table>
<tr><td>Title
44 pt.</td><td rowspan="2" style="text-align:center">Two Accounting Equations

By
Student's Name</td></tr>
<tr><td>Sub-title
32 pt.</td></tr>
</table>

Slide 2.   Title: Topics for Discussion
        Bulleted list: Two accounting equations
                Major account classifications
                Nature of an account
                Asset accounts
                Liability accounts
                Owners' equity accounts
                Revenue and expense accounts

Slide 3.   Title: Two Accounting Equations
        Bulleted list: Assets = Liabilities + Owners' Equity
                Revenues – Expenses = Net Income

Slide 4.   Title: Major Account Classifications
        Bulleted list: Assets are resources
                    Liabilities are obligations (debts)
                    Owners' Equity is amount of investment
                    Revenues increase net income
                    Expenses decrease net income

Slide 5.   Title: Nature of an Account
        Bulleted list: An account is a record of monetary increases or decreases
                    A manual account is a page in a ledger
                    A computer account is a file on a hard disk drive

Slide 6.   Title: Asset Accounts
        Bulleted list: Cash (on hand or in a bank account)
                    Accounts receivable (from customers)
                    Inventory (for resale to customers)
                    Supplies (for company use)
                    Land
                    Buildings (and other physical resources)
                    Patents (and other accounts that provide legal rights)

Slide 7.   Title: Liability Accounts
        Bulleted list: Notes payable (to banks and other creditors)
                    Accounts payable (to suppliers)
                    Wages payable (to employees)
                    Income taxes payable (to federal and state governments)

Slide 8.   Title: Owners' Equity Accounts
        Bulleted list: Common stock (paid-in capital)
                    Retained earnings (not paid to stockholders)
                    Dividends (paid to stockholders)

Slide 9.   Title: Revenue and Expense Accounts
        Bulleted list: Sales revenue (retail price of goods sold)
                    Service revenue (for work performed)
                    Cost of goods sold (largest expense)
                    Advertising expense (and other expenses)

Note: Complete slide #10 by entering one asset, liability, owners' equity, revenue, and expense account. Your opinion is important here!

Slide 10.   Title: Conclusion
        Bulleted list: Most important asset account = _____
                    Most important liability account = _____
                    Most important owners' equity account = _____
                    Most important revenue account = _____
                    Most important expense account = _____

Slide 11. Title: That's All, Folks!

The speech part of the 11-slide presentation is as follows:

1. Ladies and Gentlemen: My name is Student Name. Today, I am going to discuss two accounting equations. I am also going to classify major accounts that are used by Student's Name Corporation.

2. This means that I am going to define the parts of the accounting equations. I am also going to discuss the nature of an account. Then, I am going to classify typical asset, liability, owners' equity, revenue and expense accounts.

3. One accounting equation for my corporation is Assets = Liabilities + Owners' Equity. The other accounting equation is Revenues – Expenses = Net Income.

4. Assets are _____. Liabilities are _____. Owners' equity is _____. Revenues _____. Expenses _____.

5. In my corporation, we say an account is a record of increases and decreases in the dollar amount associated with a specific resource or activity. When our records were kept by hand, the account was a page in our ledger. Now that we keep records using computers, the account is a file on a hard disk drive.

6. Asset accounts are listed in order of liquidity in my corporation. Cash is first because it is the most liquid asset. Accounts receivable are _____. Inventory shows the cost of merchandise that we have for sale. Supplies are used by company personnel. Land, buildings, and equipment are also called plant assets. Patents, trademarks, and goodwill are legal rights owned by my corporation.

7. Most liability account names include the word "payable." Notes payable are _____. Accounts payable usually come from suppliers' invoices. Wages payable are employee related. Income taxes payable are based upon the earnings of my corporation.

8. Owners' equity accounts concern the amount of investment. Common stock shows what investors paid for ownership rights in my corporation. Retained earnings are profits that have not been paid out in dividends. Dividends are current-year cash payments to stockholders out of corporate profits.

9. Revenue accounts show increases in net income. Sales revenue shows the retail price of goods sold to our customers. Service revenue shows the fees earned for work we performed for our customers. Expense accounts show decreases in net income. Cost of goods sold, our largest expense, shows the wholesale price of merchandise sold to our customers. Advertising expense and other expenses represent the rest of our cost of doing business.

10. In conclusion, there are many important accounts in Student's Name Corporation. Some are more important than others. The most important asset account is _____ because _____. The most important liability account is _____ because _____. The most important owners' equity account is _____ because _____. The most important revenue account is _____ because _____. The most important expense account is _____ because _____.

11. Thanks for listening. Do you have any questions?

Required

Make sure that you complete the following steps in order. Refer to the procedures in the Appendix, which are alphabetized by underlined verb. Note the underlined verbs in the steps below.

1. <u>Open</u> *PowerPoint* and create a *title slide* using the data in the exhibit on page 2-1.
2. <u>Apply</u> a slide color scheme.
3. <u>Insert</u> a *bulleted list* format for slides 2 through 10.
4. <u>Insert</u> a *title only* format for slide 11.
5. <u>Apply</u> *dissolve* as a slide transition effect for slides 2 through 11.
6. <u>Apply</u> *fly from bottom* as text preset animation for slides 2 through 10.
7. <u>Apply</u> *speech text* to slides 1 through 11. Refer to Chapter 2 in your textbook to complete the speech.
8. <u>Insert</u> footers on the notes pages.
9. <u>Save</u> your project to a floppy disk.
10. Print the presentation as *notes pages*.
11. Staple the Transmittal Sheet on top of the notes pages.
12. List (on the Transmittal Sheet) accounts used in your speech and identify the financial statement in which each appears.

Project Two Transmittal Sheet

Student Name: _____

Student Identification Number: _____

Class: _____

Date: _____

_____
_____
_____
_____
_____
_____
_____
_____
_____
_____
_____
_____
_____
_____
_____
_____
_____
_____
_____
_____
_____
_____

Notes:

Project Three

Recording Business Transactions

Competencies

- Use *Microsoft®* *Excel* to create two worksheets that illustrate the recording of financing, investing, and operating activities.
- Summarize the cash flows from financing, investing, and operating activities of a corporation.

Project Data

Chart of Accounts	
Balance Sheet	**Income statement**
Cash	Sales revenue
Accounts receivable	Cost of goods sold
Inventory	Advertising expense
Equipment	Insurance expense
Furniture	Interest expense
Notes payable	Office supplies expense
Accounts payable	Rent expense
Payroll taxes payable	Repairs expense
Common stock	Salary expense
Dividends	Utilities expense

Sample Transaction

My corporation pays $5,000 rent to the landlord.

How transaction recorded using the following format:

Account	Balance Sheet				Income Statement	
Names	Cash +	Other Assets	= Liab.	+ Equity	+ Revenues	- Expenses
Rent expense						(5,000)
Cash	(5,000)					

Sheet 1. Financing activity and investing activity transactions

	A	B	C	D	E	F	G	H	I
1									
2				STUDENT'S NAME CORPORATION					
3				RECORDING BUSINESS TRANSACTIONS					
4				TODAY'S DATE					
5									

Typical financing activity transactions

a. My corporation issues $120,000 worth of stock to investors in exchange for cash.

Account		Balance Sheet				Income Statement	
Names	Cash +	Other Assets	= Liab.	+ Equity	+ Revenues	- Expenses

b. My corporation borrows $64,000 from the bank for one year.

Account		Balance Sheet				Income Statement	
Names	Cash +	Other Assets	= Liab.	+ Equity	+ Revenues	- Expenses

c. My corporation pays cash dividends to stockholders, $9,000.

Account		Balance Sheet				Income Statement	
Names	Cash +	Other Assets	= Liab.	+ Equity	+ Revenues	- Expenses

Typical investing activity transactions

d. My corporation purchases furniture for $44,000 cash.

Account		Balance Sheet				Income Statement	
Names	Cash +	Other Assets	= Liab.	+ Equity	+ Revenues	- Expenses

e. My corporation returns furniture for a $3,800 cash refund.

Account		Balance Sheet				Income Statement	
Names	Cash +	Other Assets	= Liab.	+ Equity	+ Revenues	- Expenses

Project 3, Student's Name, Identification Number, Class Number, Today's Date

Sheet 2. Operating activity transactions

STUDENT'S NAME CORPORATION
RECORDING BUSINESS TRANSACTIONS
TODAY'S DATE

Typical operating activity transactions

f. My corporation purchases $87,000 inventory on account (with intention to pay later).

Account	Balance Sheet				Income Statement	
Names	Cash +	Other Assets	= Liab.	+ Equity	+ Revenues	- Expenses

g. My corporation pays $75,000 on account.

Account	Balance Sheet				Income Statement	
Names	Cash +	Other Assets	= Liab.	+ Equity	+ Revenues	- Expenses

h. My corporation sells $60,000 worth of merchandise--$52,000 for cash and $8,000 on account.

Account	Balance Sheet				Income Statement	
Names	Cash +	Other Assets	= Liab.	+ Equity	+ Revenues	- Expenses

i. My corporation records the cost of goods sold in the above transaction, $48,000.

Account	Balance Sheet				Income Statement	
Names	Cash +	Other Assets	= Liab.	+ Equity	+ Revenues	- Expenses

j. My corporation pays employee's salary--gross pay, $1,800; deductions, $200; net pay, $1,600.

Account	Balance Sheet				Income Statement	
Names	Cash +	Other Assets	= Liab.	+ Equity	+ Revenues	- Expenses
Salary expense						
Payroll taxes payable						
Cash						

Project 3, Student's Name, Identification Number, Class Number, Today's Date

-3.3-

Required

Make sure that you complete the following steps in order. Refer to the procedures in the Appendix, which are alphabetized by underlined verb. Note the underlined verbs in the steps below.

1. <u>Open</u> *Excel* and create two worksheets to look like the examples in the project. <u>Enter</u> the date as text in cell A4. <u>Merge and center</u> the text in rows 2, 3, 4, and 45 of each worksheet. <u>Apply</u> borders in the journal (cell range B10 – H13). Copy (cell range B10 – H13) and paste it to cells B17, B24, B33, and B40 on Sheet 1. Also, paste it to cells B10, B17, B24, B32, and B39 on Sheet 2.
2. Record each transaction in a manner similar to the sample transaction. Use the account names in the chart of accounts on page 3.1. <u>Enter and format</u> the numbers. Refer to Chapter 3 in your textbook for ideas about recording the transactions.
3. <u>Format</u> each worksheet. Do not click in the Gridlines box.
4. <u>Save</u> your project to a floppy disk.
5. <u>Print</u> the *Excel* workbook.
6. Summarize by hand (on the Transmittal Sheet) the cash flows from the financing, investing, and operating activity transactions that you recorded in the cash columns on your worksheets. Refer to page 106 in your textbook for an example of a statement of cash flows.
7. Staple the Transmittal Sheet on top of the two worksheets.

Project Three Transmittal Sheet

Student Name: _____

Student Identification Number: _____

Class: _____

Date: _____

_____
_____
_____
_____
_____
_____
_____
_____
_____
_____
_____
_____
_____
_____
_____
_____
_____
_____
_____
_____
_____
_____
_____
_____
_____

Notes:

Project Four (a)

Transaction Analysis

Competencies

- Integrate *Microsoft*® *Excel* and *Microsoft*® *PowerPoint* to create a presentation that explains the rules of debit and credit and demonstrates transaction analysis.
- Demonstrate how the transactions discussed in the presentation are posted to a ledger.

Project Data

Sheet 1. Be aware of the column widths when you create the worksheet below:

A	B	C	D	E	F	G	H	I	J	K	L	M
1												
2	**Assets**		**=**	**Liabilities**		**+**	**Equity**			**+ Net Income**		
3												
4	**+**	**-**		**-**	**+**		**-**	**+**		**-**	**+**	
5												
6	**Debit**	**Credit**		**Debit**	**Credit**		**Debit**	**Credit**		**Debit**	**Credit**	
7												
8												

Sheet 2. This modified journal will be used for illustrating transactions:

	A	B	C	D	E	F	G
1	**Identify And Enter**	**Determine Financial Stmt. Effects**				**Enter Amounts As**	
2	**Account Names**	**A =**	**L +**	**E +**	**NI**	**Debits**	**Credits**
3	Advertising expense				-	1,200	
4	Accounts payable		+				1,200

Use only the following account names in this presentation:

Cash
Accounts receivable
Accounts payable
Service revenue
Advertising expense

An exhibit of slide 1 and an outline for the ten remaining slides of a presentation are as follows:

How to Analyze Transactions

By
Student's Name

Title
44 pt.

Sub-title
32 pt.

Slide 2.　　　Title: Topics for Discussion
　　　Bulleted list: Essential conditions for a transaction
　　　　　　　　Rules of debit and credit
　　　　　　　　Steps in transaction analysis
　　　　　　　　Transaction analysis demonstrations

Slide 3.　　　Title: Essential Conditions For a Transaction
　　　Bulleted list: Offer and acceptance
　　　　　　　　Exchange between buyer and seller
　　　　　　　　Measurable change in accounting equation

Slide 4.　　　Title: Rules of Debit and Credit

　　　　　　　　[Copy Sheet 1, cells A1 through M8,
　　　　　　　　　and paste onto Slide 4]

Slide 5.　　　Title: Steps in Transaction Analysis
　　　Bulleted list: Identify and enter accounts
　　　　　　　　Determine financial statement effects
　　　　　　　　Enter amounts as debits or credits

Slide 6.   Title: Demonstration 1: $1,200 worth of advertising is purchased on account (Invoice #951).

[Copy Sheet 2, cells A1 through G4, and paste onto Slide 6]

Slide 7.   Title: Demonstration 2: A client is billed $4,500 for service rendered (Invoice #3108).

[Copy Sheet 2, modified by the above transaction information, and paste onto Slide 7]

Slide 8.   Title: Demonstration 3: Check #753 for $3,000 is received on account from a client.

[Copy Sheet 2, modified by the above transaction information, and paste onto Slide 8]

Slide 9.   Title: Demonstration 4: A vendor is paid $2,000 on account with check #654.

[Copy Sheet 2, modified by the above transaction information, and paste onto Slide 9]

Slide 10.   Title: Topics Discussed
        Bulleted list: Essential conditions for a transaction
                         Rules of debit and credit
                         Steps in transaction analysis
                         Transaction analysis demonstrations

Slide 11.   Title: That's All, Folks!

Speech text:

1. Ladies and Gentlemen: Today I am going to discuss how to analyze transactions.

2. My topics include essential conditions for a transaction, rules of debit and credit, and steps in transaction analysis. I am also going to demonstrate some transactions by using a journal that is modified for educational purposes.

3. There are three essential conditions for a transaction. The first condition is that there must be an offer from a buyer and an acceptance by a seller. The second condition is that an exchange must happen between buyer and seller. The third condition is that there must be a measurable change in the accounting equation.

4. Measurable changes are recorded using debits and credits. The debit columns shown are left-hand monetary columns. The credit columns are right-hand monetary columns. Increases in assets are recorded as debits. Increases in liabilities, owners' equity, and net income are recorded as credits. The reverse is true for decreases. Revenues are increases in net income. Expenses are decreases in net income.

5. There are three steps in transaction analysis. First, identify and enter two or more accounts that are affected by the transaction. Second, determine the financial statement effect on each account line. Third, enter the dollar amounts according to the rules of debit and credit.

6. In demonstration 1, I identified and entered Advertising Expense and Accounts Payable from the key words *advertising* and *purchased on account*. Advertising Expense is a net income account. Expenses decrease net income. A decrease in net income is recorded as a debit. Accounts Payable is a liability account. More money is owed as a result of this transaction, so liabilities increase. An increase in liabilities is recorded as a credit.

7. In demonstration 2, I identified and entered…(Complete this paragraph)

8. In demonstration 3, I identified and entered…(Complete this paragraph)

9. In demonstration 4, I identified and entered…(Complete this paragraph)

10. In conclusion, I discussed essential conditions for a transaction, rules of debit and credit, and steps in transaction analysis. I also demonstrated four examples of transaction analysis.

11. Thank you for your attention. Are there any questions?

Required

Make sure that you complete the steps on the next page in order. Refer to the procedures in the Appendix, which are alphabetized by underlined verb. Note the underlined verbs in the steps.

1. Open *Excel* and create the two worksheets illustrated. Use *Times New Roman* as a font for all words and numbers. The font should be size 18 or 22. All words, symbols, and numbers should be bold. Format the numbers as shown.
2. Apply borders in each *Excel* worksheet.
3. Apply colors in each *Excel* worksheet. The fill color should be yellow. The font color should be blue.
4. Open *PowerPoint* and create a *title slide* using the data in the exhibit.
5. Apply a slide color scheme.
6. Insert a *bulleted list* format for slides 2 and 3.
7. Insert a *title only* format for slide 4. Insert the first worksheet cell range A1 – M8 into this slide.
8. Insert a *bulleted list* format for slide 5.
9. Insert a *title only* format for slides 6 – 9. Insert the second worksheet cell range A1 – G4 into slide 6. The worksheet should be modified to reflect the transaction information before inserting it into slides 7 – 9.
10. Insert a *bulleted list* format for slide 10.
11. Insert a *title only* format for slide 11.
12. Apply *dissolve* as a slide transition effect for slides 2 – 11.
13. Apply *fly from bottom* as text preset animation for slides 2, 3, 5, and 10.
14. Apply *speech text* to slides 1 - 11. Use Chapter 4 in the textbook to complete the speech.
15. Insert footers on the *notes pages*.
16. Save your project to a floppy disk.
17. A ledger page is illustrated the next page. Recreate it by hand on the Transmittal Sheet. Demonstrate how the transaction amounts discussed in the presentation are posted to the ledger you created on the Transmittal Sheet. Assume that all transactions occur today (TM/TD/TY = this month/this day/this year). ROA means received on account. POA means paid on account.
18. Print the presentation as *notes pages*.
19. Staple the Transmittal Sheet on the front of the notes pages.

The Ledger Page:

Today's Date	Account Name / Account Activity	Posted Amounts		Account Balances	
		Debit	Credit	Debit	Credit
	Cash				
TM/TD/TY	Beginning balance			8,500	
TM/TD/TY	ROA--Check #753	3,000		11,500	
TM/TD/TY	POA--Check #654		2,000	9,500	
	Accounts Receivable				
TM/TD/TY	Beginning balance			13,200	
TM/TD/TY	Sale--Invoice #3108				
TM/TD/TY	ROA--Check #753				
	Accounts payable				
TM/TD/TY	Beginning balance				7,700
TM/TD/TY	Purchase--Invoice #951				
TM/TD/TY	POA--Check #654				
	Service Revenue				
TM/TD/TY	Beginning balance				88,000
TM/TD/TY	Sale--Invoice #3108				
	Advertising Expense				
TM/TD/TY	Beginning balance			5,600	
TM/TD/TY	Purchase--Invoice #951				

Project Four (a) Transmittal Sheet

Student Name: _____

Student Identification Number: _____

Class: _____

Date: _____

_____
_____
_____
_____
_____
_____
_____
_____
_____
_____
_____
_____
_____
_____
_____
_____
_____
_____
_____
_____
_____
_____

Notes:

Project Four (b)

Adjusting Entries

Competencies

- Integrate *Microsoft®* *Excel* and *Microsoft®* *PowerPoint* to create a presentation that illustrates how adjusting entries are used in accrual accounting.
- Complete a worksheet that shows the transition from unadjusted account balances to adjusted account balances.

Project Data

This end-of-month adjustments worksheet will be completed on the transmittal sheet.

STUDENT'S NAME CORPORATION
END-OF-MONTH ADJUSTMENTS
JANUARY 31, THIS YEAR

Account Names	Unadjusted Balances		Adjustments		Adjusted Balances	
	Debit	Credit	Debit	Credit	Debit	Credit
Cash	48,000					
Accounts receivable	36,000					
Prepaid insurance	1,800					
Other assets	900,000					
Notes payable		30,000				
Unearned rent		1,500				
Interest payable		0				
Other liabilities		45,000				
Common stock		580,000				
Retained earnings		140,000				
Rent revenue		220,000				
Service revenue		86,000				
Insurance expense	0					
Interest expense	0					
Other expenses	116,700					
Totals	1,102,500	1,102,500				

Sheet 1: This exhibit shows partially completed rows from the end-of-month adjustments worksheet illustrated on the previous page.

	A	B	C	D	E	F	G
	Account	Unadjusted Balances		Adjustments		Adjusted Balances	
1		Debit	Credit	Debit	Credit	Debit	Credit
2	Names						
3	Accounts receivable	36,000		2,000		38,000	
4	Service revenue		86,000		2,000		88,000
5	Account	Unadjusted Balances		Adjustments		Adjusted Balances	
6	Names	Debit	Credit	Debit	Credit	Debit	Credit
7	Unearned rent		1,500				
8	Rent revenue		220,000				
9	Account	Unadjusted Balances		Adjustments		Adjusted Balances	
10	Names	Debit	Credit	Debit	Credit	Debit	Credit
11	Interest payable		0				
12	Interest expense	0					
13	Account	Unadjusted Balances		Adjustments		Adjusted Balances	
14	Names	Debit	Credit	Debit	Credit	Debit	Credit
15	Prepaid insurance	1,800					
16	Insurance expense	0					

An exhibit of Slide 1 and an outline for the 13 remaining slides of a presentation are as follows:

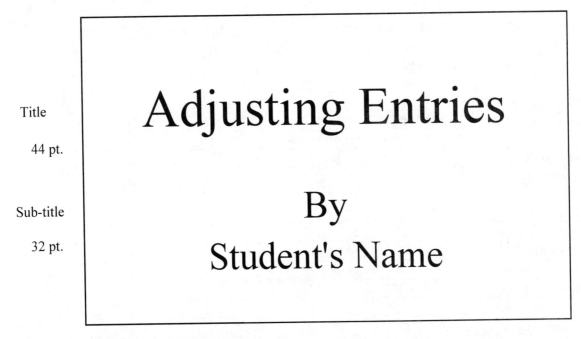

Title

44 pt.

Sub-title

32 pt.

Adjusting Entries

By

Student's Name

Slide 2.　　　Title: Topics For Discussion
　　Bulleted list: Why adjusting entries are needed
　　　　　　How rules of debit and credit are used with adjusting entries
　　　　　　Four typical adjusting entries

Slide 3.   Title: Why Adjusting Entries Are Needed

Bulleted list: Some revenues are earned before cash is received
Other revenues are earned after cash is received
Some expenses occur before cash is paid
Other expenses occur after cash is paid

Slide 4.   Title: How Rules of Debit and Credit Are Used with Adjusting Entries

Bulleted list: Debit balance + debit entry = larger debit balance
Debit balance – credit entry = smaller debit balance
Credit balance + credit entry = larger credit balance
Credit balance – debit entry = smaller credit balance

Slide 5.   Title: Typical Revenue Earned Before Cash Is Received

Sub-title: Student's Name Corporation agrees to provide $2,000 worth of services per month for three months, beginning on the first day of this month. Customer agrees to pay $6,000 when the services are complete.

Slide 6.   Title: End-of-Month Adjustment

[Insert Sheet 1, cell range A1 – G4, here]

Slide 7.   Title: Typical Revenue Earned After Cash Is Received

Sub-title: Customer agrees to pay Student's Name Corporation $1,500 in advance to rent equipment for three months, beginning on the first day of this month.

Slide 8.   Title: End-of-Month Adjustment

[Complete Sheet 1, cell range A5 – G8, and insert here]

Slide 9.   Title: Typical Expense That Occurs Before Cash Is Paid

Sub-title: Student's Name Corporation borrows $30,000 from the bank on the first day of this month. The note calls for a $750 interest payment at the end of each quarter.

Slide 10.   Title: End-of-Month Adjustment

[Complete Sheet 1, cell range A9 – G12, and insert here]

Slide 11.   Title: Typical Expense That Occurs After Cash Is Paid

Sub-title: Student's Name Corporation pays $1,800 on the first day of this month for three months' worth of insurance coverage.

Slide 12.   Title: End-of-Month Adjustment

[Complete Sheet 1, cell range A13 – G16, and insert here]

Slide 13.   Title: Conclusion
Bulleted list: Adjusting entries are needed to correct account balances
Adjusted account balances show revenues when earned
and expenses when incurred
Adjusted account balances show correct financial position

Slide 14.   Title: That's All, Folks!

The speech text (partially completed) is as follows:

1. Ladies and Gentlemen: My speech today is about adjusting entries.
2. My topics include why month-end adjusting entries are needed at Student's Name Corporation and how the rules of debit and credit are used. I will also demonstrate four typical adjusting entries.
3. At Student's Name Corporation, financial statements are prepared at the end of each month. Adjusting entries are needed to correct the account balances that appear in those statements. First, adjustments are needed to record any revenues that are earned before cash is received. Second, adjusting entries are needed to record any revenues that are earned after the cash is received. Third, adjustments are needed to record any expenses that occur before the cash is paid. Fourth, adjusting entries are needed to record any expenses that occur after the cash is paid.
4. This slide shows how the rules of debit and credit are used with adjusting entries. [Paraphrase the four applications of the rules listed on Slide 4.]
5. This slide shows that revenue is earned before the cash is received. In this example, services are provided and revenue is earned over a three-month period. This customer agrees to pay $6,000 at the end of the period. At the end of this month, $2,000 worth of service revenue is earned and is receivable from the customer.
6. I selected accounts receivable and service revenue as the account names for this adjustment. The accounts receivable debit balance needs to be increased from $36,000 to $38,000 to reflect the addition. A $2,000 debit entry is used for this correction. The service revenue credit balance needs to be increased from $86,000 to $88,000 for the same reason. A $2,000 credit entry is used for this correction.
7. This slide shows that… [Explain]
8. I selected… [Explain]
9. This slide shows that… [Explain]
10. I selected… [Explain]
11. This slide shows that… [Explain]
12. I selected… [Explain]
13. In conclusion, I explained that month-end adjusting entries are needed at Student's Name Corporation to correct account balances. The adjusted account balances are used on the company's financial statements to show revenue when earned and expenses when incurred. They also show the company's proper financial position.

14. Thanks for listening! Are there any questions?

Required

> **Make sure that you complete the following steps in order. Refer to the procedures in the Appendix, which are alphabetized by underlined verb. Note the underlined verbs in the steps below.**

1. <u>Open</u> *Excel* and create the worksheet illustrated on page 4b.2. Use information in the slide outline on pages 4b.2 – 4b.4 and in the textbook to complete the worksheet.
2. <u>Apply</u> borders in the Excel worksheet. <u>Apply</u> colors in the Excel worksheet. The font color should be blue. The font letters and numbers should be bold. The fill color should be yellow.
3. <u>Open</u> *PowerPoint* and create a *title slide* using the data in the exhibit on page 4b.2.
4. <u>Apply</u> a slide color scheme (blue background).
5. <u>Insert</u> a *bulleted list* format for slides 2, 3, 4, and 13.
6. <u>Insert</u> a *title* format for slides 5, 7, 9, and 11. (The title format includes a sub-title.)
7. <u>Insert</u> a *title only* format for slides 6, 8, 10, 12, and 14. <u>Insert</u> *Excel* cell ranges into slide where indicated.
8. <u>Apply</u> dissolve as a slide transition effect for slides 2 – 14.
9. <u>Apply</u> the *fly from bottom* text preset animation for slides 2, 3, 4, and 13.
10. <u>Apply</u> *speech text* to slides 1 – 14. Complete the speech where indicated. Use Chapter 4 in the textbook as a source of information.
11. <u>Insert</u> footers on the notes pages.
12. <u>Save</u> your project to a floppy disk.
13. <u>Print</u> the presentation as *notes pages*.
14. Staple the Transmittal Sheet to the front of the notes pages.
15. Enter by hand on the Transmittal Sheet the end-of-month adjustments worksheet shown on page 4b.1. Complete the worksheet based upon the adjusting entries demonstrated in the slide presentation. The adjustments debit column total should equal the adjustments credit column total. The adjusted balances debit column total should equal the adjusted balances credit column total.

Project Four (b) Transmittal Sheet

Student Name: _____

Student Identification Number: _____

Class: _____

Date: _____

_____

_____

_____

_____

_____

_____

_____

_____

_____

_____

_____

_____

_____

_____

_____

_____

_____

_____

_____

_____

_____

Notes:

Project Five

Financial Statements

Competencies

- Integrate *Microsoft® Excel* and *Microsoft® Word* to create and summarize the information in an income statement, statement of stockholders' equity, and balance sheet.
- Demonstrate the effects of a transaction on total assets, total liabilities, stockholders' equity, and net income.

Project Data

Notes:

1. The list of accounts and their balances in sheet 1 (next page) is based upon Exhibit 1 shown in Chapter 5 of the textbook. When the account balances are shown as debits and credits, the list is also known as an adjusted trial balance. The adjusted trial balance is the source of account balances in three of the financial statements. The financial statements are linked to the adjusted trial balance and to each other with cell-based formulas. When the amounts are changed on the adjusted trial balance, the amounts in the financial statements change automatically.

2. The list of accounts is in financial statement order if the balance sheet is created first. In actual practice, however, the income statement is usually created first and the balance sheet is created last.

3. The effects of a transaction will be demonstrated on the Transmittal Sheet using the following table:

Reported On Financial Statements	Totals Before Transaction	Totals After Transaction
Net income................	$194,000	
Total assets...............	$4,364,000	
Total liabilities............	$2,380,000	
Stockholders' equity.....	1,984,000	
Total liabilities plus stockholders' equity...	$4,364,000	

Sheet 1. Use sum functions to create the column totals in cells C29 and D29.

	A	B	C	D	E
1					
2		STUDENT'S NAME CORPORATION			
3		ADJUSTED TRIAL BALANCE			
4		DECEMBER 31, THIS YEAR			
5					
6		ACCOUNT NAMES	DEBITS	CREDITS	
7					
8		Cash	164,000		
9		Accounts receivable	270,000		
10		Merchandise inventory	430,000		
11		Other current assets	158,000		
12		Equipment	4,080,000		
13		Accumulated depreciation		1,060,000	
14		Goodwill	322,000		
15		Accounts payable		265,000	
16		Other current liabilities		171,000	
17		Notes payable, current portion		144,000	
18		Notes payable, long-term		1,800,000	
19		Common stock		1,200,000	
20		Retained earnings, beg. balance		640,000	
21		Dividends	50,000		
22		Sales revenue		1,900,000	
23		Cost of goods sold	740,000		
24		Salaries and wages expense	375,000		
25		Other operating expenses	422,000		
26		Interest expense	103,000		
27		Income tax expense	66,000		
28					
29		**Totals**	**7,180,000**	**7,180,000**	
30					
31		Shares of stock outstanding	1,200,000		
32					
33		Project 5, Student's Name, Identification Number, Class Number, Today's Date			

Sheet 2. Use cell-based formulas or functions to create all amounts shown.

	A	B	C	D
1				
2		STUDENT'S NAME CORPORATION		
3		INCOME STATEMENT		
4		YEAR ENDED DECEMBER 31, THIS YEAR		
5				
6		**Sales revenue**..	**$1,900,000**	
7		Cost of goods sold..	740,000	
8				
9		**Gross profit**...	**1,160,000**	
10		Operating expenses		
11		Salaries and wages...	375,000	
12		Other operating expenses..	422,000	
13				
14		Total operating expenses...	797,000	
15				
16		**Operating income**...	**363,000**	
17		Interest expense...	103,000	
18				
19		Pretax income...	260,000	
20		Income taxes expense..	66,000	
21				
22		**Net income**...	**$194,000**	
23				
24		**Earnings per share of common stock**............................	**$0.16**	
25				
26		Project 5, Student's Name, Identification Number, Class Number, Today's Date		

Sheet 3. Use cell-based formulas or functions to create all amounts shown.

	A	B	C	D	E	F
1						
2		STUDENT'S NAME CORPORATION				
3		STATEMENT OF STOCKHOLDERS' EQUITY				
4		YEAR ENDED DECEMBER 31, THIS YEAR				
5						
6			Common	Retained		
7			Stock	Earnings	TOTAL	
8						
9		Beginning balances.....................	$1,200,000	$640,000	$1,840,000	
10		Net income.....................................		194,000	194,000	
11		Dividends paid................................		(50,000)	(50,000)	
12						
13		**Ending balances**.......................	**$1,200,000**	**$784,000**	**$1,984,000**	
14						
15		**Dividends per share of common stock**.................................			**$0.04**	
16						
17		Project 5, Student's Name, Identification Number, Class Number, Today's Date				

Sheet 4. Use cell-based formulas or functions to create all amounts shown.

	A	B	C	D
1				
2		STUDENT'S NAME CORPORATION		
3		BALANCE SHEET		
4		DECEMBER 31, THIS YEAR		
5				
6		ASSETS		
7		Current assets		
8		Cash..	$164,000	
9		Accounts receivable....................................	270,000	
10		Merchandise inventory.................................	430,000	
11		Other current assets....................................	158,000	
12				
13		Total current assets....................................	1,022,000	
14		**Property, plant, and equipment**		
15		Equipment...	4,080,000	
16		Less: accumulated depreciation...................	1,060,000	
17				
18		Property, plant, and equipment, net..............	3,020,000	
19		**Other assets:**		
20		Goodwill..	322,000	
21				
22		**Total assets..**	**$4,364,000**	
23				
24		LIABILITIES AND STOCKHOLDERS' EQUITY		
25		**Current liabilities**		
26		Accounts payable...	$265,000	
27		Other current liabilities................................	171,000	
28		Notes payable, current portion......................	144,000	
29				
30		Total current liabilities.................................	580,000	
31		**Long-term liabilities**		
32		Notes payable, long-term..............................	1,800,000	
33		**Stockholders' equity**		
34		Common stock, 5,000,000 shares authorized,		
35		1,200,000 shares outstanding....................	1,200,000	
36		Retained earnings, ending balance................	784,000	
37				
38		Total stockholders' equity............................	1,984,000	
39				
40		**Total liabilities and stockholders' equity........**	**$4,364,000**	
41				
42		Project 5, Student's Name, Identification Number, Class Number, Today's Date		

Report text (partially completed):

Financial Statements
By
Student's Name

If you are new to investing, this report will be helpful to you. The report discusses the information in three financial statements that are in the Student's Name Corporation annual report. The financial statements are the income statement, the statement of stockholders' equity, and the balance sheet.

First, is the income statement. This statement is defined as…(complete the sentence).

[Insert Sheet 2, cells A1 – D26, *as a picture*]

Key figures in the income statement are for sales revenue, gross profit, operating income, net income, and earnings per share. Sales revenue, $1,900,000, is…(complete the sentence). Gross profit… Operating income… Net income… Earnings per share…

Second is the statement of stockholders' equity. This statement is defined as…

[Insert Sheet 3, cells A1 – F17, *as a picture*]

This statement shows what contributes to the ending balances for common stock and retained earnings. Common stock, $1,200,000, is…(complete the sentence). Retained earnings are… This statement also shows a $0.04 dividend per share of common stock. The focus of this company is on growth, not dividend payments.

The third statement is the balance sheet. This statement is defined as…

The assets section of the balance sheet shows key figures for current assets; property, plant, and equipment; and other assets. Current assets, $1,022,000, are… Property, plant, and equipment, $3,020,000, are… Other assets are…

The liabilities section shows key figures for current liabilities and long-term debt. Current liabilities, $580,000, are… Long-term liabilities, $1,800,000, are…

The stockholders' equity section shows key figures for common stock and retained earnings. The total of stockholders' equity plus current and long-term liabilities is equal to total assets. The balance sheet reflects the accounting equation.

[Insert Sheet 4, cells A1 – D42, *as a picture*]

The two most important amounts in the financial statements are…(description and dollars) and…(description and dollars). They are important because…

Required

1. Open *Excel*. Insert a fourth worksheet into the workbook.
2. Create four worksheets that look like the examples in this project. Merge and center the text in the heading and the bottom row of each worksheet. Enter the date as text in the balance sheet. Enter a cell-based formula or function to calculate each amount in the three financial statements. Format each worksheet. Do not use gridlines.
3. Open *Word* and create a report based upon the partially completed text in this project and upon information in Chapter 5 of the textbook. Complete all sentences. The report should be for rookie investors so that they can better read your company's annual report. Insert each *Excel* cell range (financial statement) into the *Word* document *as a picture*.
4. Insert footers into the *Word* document.
5. Save your project to a floppy disk.
6. Print the *Word* document.
7. Copy worksheets 2 – 4.
8. Print each worksheet copy to show the formulas.
9. Staple each worksheet copy to the back of the report.
10. Staple the Transmittal Sheet to the front of the report.
11. Create by hand on the Transmittal Sheet the table on page 5.1. Change the balances of four accounts on Sheet 1 by the amounts in the following transaction:

    Assume that $10,000 worth of merchandise is sold on account. The merchandise cost Student's Name Corporation $4,000.

    Record on the Transmittal Sheet the after-transaction totals from the income statement (Sheet 2) and balance sheet (Sheet 4).

Project Five Transmittal Sheet

Student Name: _____

Student Identification Number: _____

Class: _____

Date: _____

_____
_____
_____
_____
_____
_____
_____
_____
_____
_____
_____
_____
_____
_____
_____
_____
_____
_____
_____
_____
_____
_____
_____

Notes:

Project Six

Interpreting Cash Flows

Competencies

- Integrate *Microsoft® Excel* and *Microsoft® PowerPoint* to create a presentation that interprets the cash flow data from four hypothetical corporations.
- Create the operating activities section of a statement of cash flows using the indirect format.

Project Data

Sheet 1. The cash flow data from a growth company.

Cash flow data (in thousands)	This Year	Last Year	Prev. Year
Cash provided by operating activities...	$550,000	$474,000	$408,000
Cash used for investing activities.........	(850,000)	(733,000)	(632,000)
Cash provided by financing activities...	450,000	388,000	334,000
Net increase in cash...........................	$150,000	$129,000	$110,000

Sheet 2. The cash flow data from a prosperous company that is growing slowly.

Cash flow data (in thousands)	This Year	Last Year	Prev. Year
Cash provided by operating activities...	$350,000	$340,000	$330,000
Cash used for investing activities.........	(100,000)	(97,000)	(94,000)
Cash used for financing activities.........	(200,000)	(194,000)	(188,000)
Net increase in cash...........................	$50,000	$49,000	$48,000

Sheet 3. The cash flow data from a company that is struggling to pay its long-term debt.

	A	B		C	D	E	F
1							
2		Cash flow data (in thousands)		This	Last	Prev.	
3				Year	Year	Year	
4		Cash provided by operating activities...		$156,000	$182,000	$235,000	
5		Cash provided by investing activities...		248,000	276,000	275,000	
6		Cash used for financing activities.........		(400,000)	(450,000)	(500,000)	
7							
8		Net increase in cash..........................		$4,000	$8,000	$10,000	
9							

Sheet 4. The cash flow data from a company that is moving toward insolvency.

	A	B		C	D	E	F
1							
2		Cash flow data (in thousands)		This	Last	Prev.	
3				Year	Year	Year	
4		Cash used for operating activities.........		($98,000)	($84,000)	($72,000)	
5		Cash provided by investing activities...		80,000	40,000	0	
6		Cash provided by financing activities...		22,000	50,000	80,000	
7							
8		Net increase in cash..........................		$4,000	$6,000	$8,000	
9							

An exhibit of Slide 1 and an outline for the 11 remaining slides of a presentation are as follows:

Title
44 pt.

Sub-title
32 pt.

Interpreting Cash Flows

By
Student's Name

Slide 2.   Title: Topics For Discussion
         Bulleted list: Statement of cash flows
                        Why statement sections are analyzed
                        Cash flow data from four corporations

Slide 3.   Title: Statement of Cash Flows
         Bulleted list: Purpose of statement
                        Operating activities section
                        Investing activities section
                        Financing activities section

Slide 4.   Title: Why Statement Sections Are Analyzed
         Bulleted list: To account for the difference between net income (loss)
                            and cash inflow (outflow)
                        To see the cash impact of investing and financing decisions
                        To see if the corporation is dealing with serious financial problems

Slide 5.   Title: Cash Flow Data from Four Corporations
         Bulleted list: Growth company
                        Prosperous company
                        Struggling company
                        Insolvent company

Slide 6.   Title: Growth Company Example

                [Insert Sheet 1, cell range A1 – F9, here]

Slide 7.   Title: Prosperous Company Example

                [Insert Sheet 2, cell range A1 – F9, here]

Slide 8.   Title: Struggling Company Example

                [Insert Sheet 3, cell range A1 – F9, here]

Slide 9.   Title: Insolvent Company Example

                [Insert Sheet 4, cell range A1 – F9, here]

Slide 10.   Title: Topics For Discussion
         Bulleted list: Statement of cash flows
                        Why statement sections are analyzed
                        Cash flow data from four corporations

Slide 11.   Title: That's All, Folks!

The speech text (partially completed) is as follows:

1. Ladies and gentlemen: My speech today is about interpreting cash flows.

2. First, I will discuss the purpose of the statement of cash flows. Second, I will discuss why the operating, investing, and financing activities sections are analyzed. Third, I will interpret the cash flow data from four hypothetical corporations.

3. The statement of cash flows is one of four financial statements found in the annual report of a corporation. The purpose of the statement is... [Explain] The operating activities section shows... [Explain] The investing activities section shows... [Explain] The financing activities section shows...[Explain]

4. There are several reasons why the sections of the statement of cash flows are analyzed. [Give three reasons]

5. I will now interpret the cash flow data from four hypothetical corporations. First, I will discuss a company that is growing by more than 15% per year. Second, I will discuss a prosperous company that is not growing very rapidly. Third, I will discuss a company that is struggling to pay off its long-term debt. Fourth, I will interpret the data of a company that appears to be moving toward insolvency.

6. This slide shows the cash flow data from a growth company. Cash provided by operating activities is increasing by more than 15% per year. The company is growing because the management is investing in new long-term assets. The management is financing the asset acquisitions with cash provided by operating and financing activities.

7. This slide shows the cash flow data from a prosperous company that is not growing very rapidly. [Explain the data]

8. This slide shows the cash flow data from a company that is struggling to pay its long-term debt. [Explain the data]

9. This slide shows the cash flow data from a company that is moving toward insolvency. The term *insolvency* means the company does not have enough cash to pay its debts. [Explain the data]

10. In conclusion, I discussed the purpose of the statement of cash flows and why statement sections are analyzed. I then interpreted the cash flow data from four hypothetical corporations.

11. Thanks for listening! Are there any questions?

Required

1. <u>Open</u> *Excel* and create the worksheets illustrated.
2. <u>Apply</u> borders and colors to the worksheets. The font size should be 18 point.
3. <u>Open</u> *PowerPoint* and create a *title slide* using the data in the exhibit on page 6.2.
4. <u>Apply</u> a slide color scheme (blue background).
5. <u>Insert</u> a *bulleted list* format for slides 2 – 5 and 10.
6. <u>Insert</u> a *title only* format for slides 6 – 9, and 13. Insert worksheet cell ranges as indicated.
7. <u>Apply</u> *dissolve* as a slide transition effect for slides 2 – 11.
8. <u>Apply</u> the *fly from bottom* text preset animation for slides 2 – 5 and 10.
9. <u>Apply</u> *speech text* to slides 1 – 11. Use Chapter 6 in the textbook as a source of information. Exhibit 7 is especially helpful.
10. <u>Insert</u> footers on the notes pages.
11. <u>Save</u> your project to a floppy disk.
12. <u>Print</u> the presentation as *notes pages*.
13. Staple the Transmittal Sheet to the front of the notes pages.
14. Create (by hand on the Transmittal Sheet) the operating activities section of a statement of cash flows using the indirect format. Indicate the net cash provided by or used for operating activities. Use the data shown below:

December 31............................	Last Year	This Year
Accounts receivable.....................	$430,000	$473,000
Other current assets....................	845,000	760,500
Accounts payable.......................	380,000	418,000
Other current liabilities.................	420,000	378,000

Year ended December 31............................	This Year
Net income...	$939,000
Depreciation expense................................	378,000

Project Six Transmittal Sheet

Student Name: _____

Student Identification Number: _____

Class: _____

Date: _____

_____
_____
_____
_____
_____
_____
_____
_____
_____
_____
_____
_____
_____
_____
_____
_____
_____
_____
_____
_____
_____
_____
_____

Notes:

Project Seven

Time Value of Money

Competencies

- Integrate *Microsoft® Excel* and *Microsoft® Word* to create a report that defines and illustrates the present and future values of money.
- Use present and future value tables to calculate investment values for various periods.

Project Data

Notes:

1. The function used in Sheet 1, cells D13 – F15, is as follows:

$$=-PV(rate,nper,pmt,fv,type)$$

Make sure that you enter the minus sign before the PV. Substitute cell addresses for rate, nper, pmt, fv, and type. The interest rates (rate) are in cells D6 – F6. The number of years (nper) are in cells D7 – F7. The annuity payment (pmt) is in cell D8. The single future value (fv) is in cell D9. The payment type (type) in cell D10 has to do with when the payment is received.

The annuity should be zero if you are looking for the present value of a single future value. The single payment should be zero if you are looking for the present value of an annuity.

2. The function used in Sheet 1 (2), cells D13 – F15, is as follows:

$$=-FV(rate,nper,pmt,pv,type)$$

Make sure that you enter the minus sign before the FV. Substitute cell addresses for rate, nper, pmt, fv, and type. The interest rates (rate) are in cells D6 – F6. The number of years (nper) are in cells D7 – F7. The annuity payment (pmt) is in cell D8. The single present value (pv) is in cell D9. The payment type (type) in cell D10 has to do with when the payment is received.

The annuity should be zero if you are looking for the future value of a single present value. The single payment should be zero if you are looking for the future value of an annuity.

Sheet 1. This worksheet shows nine possible present values of one future value.

	A	B	C	D	E	F	G
1							
2			**STUDENT'S NAME CORPORATION**				
3			**PRESENT VALUE**				
4			**TODAY'S DATE**				
5		DATA					
6			Interest rates	3%	6%	11%	
7			Number of years	20	25	30	
8			Each annuity payment	$0			
9			Single future value	$1,000,000			
10			Payment type	0	Beg. of year = 1, end of year = 0		
11		CALCULATIONS--PRESENT VALUE					
12				20	25	30	
13			3%	$553,676	$477,606	$411,987	
14			6%	$311,805	$232,999	$174,110	
15			11%	$124,034	$73,608	$43,683	
16		CHART					

Bar chart titled with legend 3%, 6%, 11%; x-axis "Years" (20, 25, 30); y-axis $0 to $600,000.

Project 7, Student's Name, Identification Number, Class Number, Today's Date

Note: The above chart shows how much you would have to invest today to receive $1,000,000 at some point in the future. There are no guarantees if you invest in a mutual fund. If you invest $43,683 today in a mutual fund that averages an 11% return, you should be a millionaire in 30 years.

Sheet 1 (2). This is a copy of Sheet 1 after appropriate changes are made.

	A	B	C	D	E	F	G
1							
2			**STUDENT'S NAME CORPORATION**				
3			**FUTURE VALUE**				
4			**TODAY'S DATE**				
5		**DATA**					
6			Interest rates	3%	6%	11%	
7			Number of years	20	25	30	
8			Each annuity payment	$2,000			
9			Single present value	$0			
10			Payment type	0	Beg. of year = 1, end of year = 0		
11		**CALCULATIONS--FUTURE VALUE**					
12				20	25	30	
13			3%	$53,741	$72,919	$95,151	
14			6%	$73,571	$109,729	$158,116	
15			11%	$128,406	$228,827	$398,042	
16		**CHART**					
17							

(Chart: Future Value bar chart)

$450,000
$400,000
$350,000
$300,000
$250,000
$200,000
$150,000
$100,000
$50,000
$0

Legend: ▨ 3% ■ 6% ☐ 11%

X-axis: 20   25   30

Years

| 34 | Project 7, Student's Name, Identification Number, Class Number, Today's Date |

Note: This chart shows how much you will have at some future date if you invest $2,000 per year for the indicated number of years. There are no guarantees if you invest in a mutual fund. If that fund averages an 11% annual return you should have approximately $398,042 in 30 years.

Required

1. <u>Open</u> *Excel* and create a worksheet with a chart that looks like *Sheet 1* on page 7.2. <u>Merge and center</u> the text in rows 2, 3, 4, and 34. <u>Enter</u> and format the dollar amounts, numbers, and percentages in the data section. <u>Enter</u> cell-based formulas and functions to calculate all amounts in rows 12 – 15. <u>Format</u> the worksheet.
2. <u>Copy</u> the worksheet. Make text changes in rows 3, 9, and 11 of *Sheet 1 (2)*. Enter the future value function in cells D13 – F15.
3. <u>Open</u> *Word* and create a single-spaced report from the information in Chapter 7 of your textbook. The report should have the title *Time Value of Money by Student's Name* and a short introduction. The main body of the report should define and illustrate the present and future value of single payments and annuities.
4. <u>Insert</u> four *Excel* worksheets, cell range A1 – G34, *as pictures* into the *Word* document based upon the following data:

Sheet 1—present value of single future value

	A	B	C	D	E	F	G
5		**DATA**					
6			Interest rates	6%	11%	16%	
7			Number of years	20	25	30	
8			Each annuity payment	$0			
9			Single future value	$1,000,000			
10			Payment type	0	Beg. of year = 1, end of year = 0		

Sheet 1—present value of an annuity

	A	B	C	D	E	F	G
5		**DATA**					
6			Interest rates	6%	11%	16%	
7			Number of years	20	25	30	
8			Each annuity payment	$1,620			
9			Single future value	$0			
10			Payment type	0	Beg. of year = 1, end of year = 0		

Sheet 1 (2)—future value of a single present value

	A	B	C	D	E	F	G
5		**DATA**					
6			Interest rates	6%	11%	16%	
7			Number of years	20	25	30	
8			Each annuity payment	$0			
9			Single present value	$11,650			
10			Payment type	0	Beg. of year = 1, end of year = 0		

Sheet 1 (2)—future value of an annuity

	A	B	C	D	E	F	G
5		**DATA**					
6			Interest rates	6%	11%	16%	
7			Number of years	20	25	30	
8			Each annuity payment	$2,000			
9			Single present value	$0			
10			Payment type	0	Beg. of year = 1, end of year = 0		

Reduce the size of the inserted worksheets so that they fit properly in the document. Cite calculated amounts from the worksheets. The conclusion should include your observations about the worksheet calculations and charts.

5. <u>Insert</u> footers into the *Word* document.
6. <u>Save</u> your project to a floppy disk.
7. <u>Print</u> the *Word* document and staple the Transmittal Sheet on top of the report.
8. Use present and future value tables in the textbook to calculate by hand on the Transmittal Sheet the following investment values:

Assume that you plan to have $1,000,000 in 25 years. How much do you have to invest today in a growth & income fund that has an 11% annual yield?

FV [$1,000,000] x Factor [_____] = PV [_____]

Assume that you plan to receive $1,620 each year for the next 20 years. How much would you have to invest today in an income fund that has a 6% yield?

Annuity [$1,620] x Factor [_____] = PV [_____]

Assume that you invest $11,650 today in a growth & income fund that has an 11% annual yield. What will your investment be worth in 25 years?

PV [$11,650] x Factor [_____] = FV [_____]

Assume that you invest $2,000 per year in an income fund that yields 6% per year. What will your investment be worth in 20 years?

Annuity [$2,000] x Factor [_____] = FV [_____]

---

9. <u>Copy</u> Sheet 1 (the original worksheet) again. The new copy should be *Sheet 1 (3)*.
10. <u>Print</u> this worksheet copy to show the formulas.
11. <u>Staple</u> Sheet 1 (3) to the back of the Transmittal Sheet behind the report.

Project Seven Transmittal Sheet

Student Name: _____

Student Identification Number: _____

Class: _____

Date: _____

_____
_____
_____
_____
_____
_____
_____
_____
_____
_____
_____
_____
_____
_____
_____
_____
_____
_____
_____
_____
_____

Notes:

Project Eight

Financing Activities

Competencies

- Integrate *Microsoft® Excel* and *Microsoft® PowerPoint* to create a presentation that explains and demonstrates long-term bonds and capital leases.
- Calculate the present values of bonds and capital leases by varying the time periods and interest rates.

Project Data

Sheet 1.   The function in cell B14 is =−PV(F7,F8,D14,0)
The function in cell B15 is =−PV(F7,F8,0,F10)
The number in cell E15 is not the result of a formula

A	B	C	D	E	F	G
1						
2		STUDENT'S NAME CORPORATION				
3		LONG-TERM BONDS				
4		DECEMBER 31, THIS YEAR				
5						
6	DATA					
7	Real (market) semiannual interest rate................. 4.00%					
8	Semiannual periods to maturity.......................... 10					
9	Stated semiannual interest rate......................... 4.25%					
10	Face value (principal amount) of bond issue......... $7,000,000					
11	CALCULATIONS					
12	Present	Type Of	Payment	Number Of	Total	
13	Values	Payment	Amount	Payments	Payments	
14	$2,412,991	Interest	$297,500	10	$2,975,000	
15	4,728,949	Principal	7,000,000	1	7,000,000	
16						
17	$7,141,941	= Cash inflow		Cash outflow =	$9,975,000	
18						
19	Project 8, Student's Name, Identification Number, Class Number, Today's Date					

Sheet 2. The formula in cell B14 is =G7+364
The function in cell C14 is =–PV(G8,G9,G10)
The formula in cell C15 is =G14

	A	B	C	D	E	F	G	H

STUDENT'S NAME CORPORATION
CAPITAL LEASE
DECEMBER 31, THIS YEAR

DATA
Lease start date..1/1/01
Rate of interest included in payment...........................9.00%...
Number of lease payments..3........
Annual lease payment..$12,000

CALCULATIONS

Years Ended	Values at Beg. of Year	Interest Expense	Future Payments	Amortization of Principal	Values at End of Year
12/31/01	$30,376	$2,734	$12,000	$9,266	$21,109
12/31/02	21,109	1,900	12,000	10,100	11,009
12/31/03	11,009	991	12,000	11,009	0
Totals		$5,624	$36,000	$30,376	

Project 8, Student's Name, Identification Number, Class Number, Today's Date

Outline of Slides 1 – 16:

Slide 1.   Title: Bonds and Capital Leases
              Sub-title: By
                         Student's Name

Slide 2.   Title: Two Sources of Financing
          Bulleted list: Long-term bonds
                         Capital lease obligations

Slide 3.   Title: Long-term Bonds
          Bulleted list: Bonds are contracts
                         Bond certificates
                         Debenture bonds
                         Mortgage (secured) bonds

Slide 4.   Title: Price of 8.00%, 5-Year Bonds
                         Issued at Par

                [Insert Sheet 1, cells A5 – G19, into Slide 4]

Slide 5.   Title: Price of 7.50%, 5-Year Bonds
                    Issued at a Discount

            [Change stated semiannual interest rate on Sheet 1 to 3.75%,
                    and insert cells A5 – G19 into Slide 5]

Slide 6.   Title: Price of 8.50%, 5-Year Bonds
                    Issued at a Premium

            [Change stated semiannual interest rate on Sheet 1 to 4.25%,
                    and insert cells A5 – G19 into Slide 6]

Slide 7.   Title: Capital Lease Obligations
            Bulleted list: Company leases resource for most of its useful life
                            Capital lease is a liability
                            Related resource is an asset

Slide 8.   Title: Present Value of 9.00%,
                    3-Year Capital Lease

            [Insert Sheet 2, cells A5 – H20, into Slide 8]

Slide 9.   Title: Present Value of 7.00%,
                    3-Year Capital Lease

            [Change the interest rate on Sheet 2 from 9.00% to 7.00%,
                    and insert cells A5 – H20 into Slide 9]

Slide 10.   Title: Conclusion
                        Two Sources of Financing
            Bulleted list: Long-term bonds
                            Capital lease obligations

Slide 11.   Title: That's All, Folks!

The speech text (partially completed) is as follows:

1. Ladies and Gentlemen: My speech today is about bonds and capital leases.
2. Long-term bonds and capital leases are two sources of financing at Student's Name Corporation.
3. Long-term bonds are contracts between... Bond certificates show when principal and interest payments are made. Debenture bonds are... Mortgage (secured) bonds are...
4. Long-term bonds can be issued at par, at a discount, or at a premium. This slide shows... [Explain key data and calculations of bonds issued at par.]
5. This slide shows... [Explain key data and calculations of bonds issued at a discount.]
6. This slide shows... [Explain key data and calculations of bonds issued at a premium.]

7. Capital lease obligations happen when Student's Name Corporation…
8. This slide shows the calculation of capital lease values. [Explain how the present value and interest expense is calculated.]
9. This slide shows the calculation of capital lease values at a lower interest rate. [Explain how a decrease in interest rate impacts the present value of the lease.]
10. In conclusion, I discussed and demonstrated two sources of financing. They were…
11. Thanks for listening! Are there any questions?

Required

> **Make sure that you complete the following steps in order. Refer to the procedures in the Appendix, which are alphabetized by underlined verb. Note the underlined verbs in the steps below.**

1. Open *Excel* and create the two worksheets illustrated. Enter and format the numbers as shown in the data section. Enter a cell-based formula for each calculation (except where noted). Use a yellow background and a blue font color. Do not format the worksheets at this time.
2. Open *PowerPoint* and create a *title slide*.
3. Apply a slide color scheme that has a blue background and a yellow font color.
4. Insert a *bulleted list* format for slides 2, 3, 7, and 10.
5. Insert a *title only* format for slides 4 – 6, 8, 9 and 11.
6. Apply *dissolve* as a slide transition effect for slides 2 – 11.
7. Apply *fly from bottom* as text preset animation for slides 2, 3, 7, and 10.
8. Apply a *speech text* to slides 1 – 11. Complete the speech as necessary. Use Chapter 8 in the textbook as a source of information.
9. Insert footers on the notes pages.
10. Save your project to a floppy disk. Copy the worksheets and format the copies.
11. Print the slides as notes pages. Print your worksheet copies to show formulas.
12. Attach the Transmittal Sheet to the front of the notes pages and worksheets to back.
13. Calculate (by hand on the Transmittal Sheet) the present values of the bonds and capital leases mentioned in the presentation. Use the tables in the textbook.

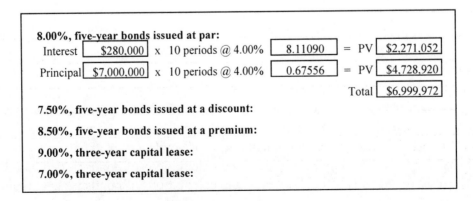

-8.4-

Project Eight Transmittal Sheet

Student Name: _____

Student Identification Number: _____

Class: _____

Date: _____

_____

_____

_____

_____

_____

_____

_____

_____

_____

_____

_____

_____

_____

_____

_____

_____

_____

_____

_____

_____

_____

_____

_____

_____

_____

_____

Notes:

Project Nine

Analysis of Financing Activities

Competencies

- Integrate *Microsoft*® *Excel* and *Microsoft*® *Word* to create a report that uses financial statement information from two corporations to evaluate their financing activities.
- Compare the cash flows of two corporations and explain which corporation appears to be a better investment from a cash flows perspective.

Project Data

Sheet 1 (partially completed)

	A	B	C	D	E	F	G	H
1								
2		STUDENT'S NAME CORPORATION						
3		FINANCING ACTIVITIES COMPARISON						
4		DECEMBER 31, THIS YEAR						
5								
6		DATA	Student's Name Corp.			Relative's Name Corp.		
7		(in millions)	This Year	Last Year		This Year	Last Year	
8								
9		Current assets	$17,300	$14,300		$9,600	$9,300	
10		Long-term assets	22,300	20,100		11,900	12,200	
11		Current liabilities	12,000	10,000		6,900	6,200	
12		Long-term debt	10,600	9,700		4,300	5,800	
13		Other long-term liabilities	700	400		300	300	
14		Common stock	200	200		200	200	
15		Paid-in capital	500	500		300	300	
16		Treasury stock	(400)	(300)		(200)	(200)	
17		Retained earnings, beg. bal.	13,900	12,200		8,900	7,700	
18		Net income (loss)	2,700	2,100		900	1,400	
19		Dividends	(600)	(400)		(100)	(200)	
20		Net operating cash flow	1,700	1,500		1,300	1,500	
21		Net investing cash flow	(2,500)	(2,400)		0	(1,800)	
22		Net financing cash flow	500	600		(1,400)	300	
23		Market value	50,400	44,200		25,300	31,800	
24								
25		CALCULATIONS						
26		Return on assets	6.8%					
27		Assets to equity ratio	2.43					
28		Return on equity	16.6%					
29		Debt to equity ratio	65.0%					
30		Debt to assets ratio	26.8%					
31		Current ratio	1.44					
32		Dividend payout ratio	22.2%					
33		Market to book value ratio	3.09					
34								
35		Project 9, Student's Name, Identification Number, Class Number, Today's Date						

Required

1. <u>Open</u> *Excel* and create a worksheet that looks like the example on page 9.1. <u>Merge and center</u> the text in rows 2, 3, 4, and 35. <u>Enter</u> and format the dollar amounts in the data section. <u>Enter</u> cell-based formulas and functions to calculate all amounts in cells C26 – G33.
2. <u>Format</u> the worksheet.
3. <u>Open</u> *Word* and create a single-spaced report from the information in Chapter 9 of your textbook. The report should have the title *Financing Activities Comparison by Student's Name* and a short introduction. <u>Insert</u> the *Excel* worksheet, cells A1 – H35, *as a picture* into the *Word* document under the introduction. The main body of the report should define each calculation and indicate which corporation is better for that calculation. Cite specific amounts from the worksheet. The conclusion should include your observations about the worksheet calculations and which corporation is a better investment.
4. <u>Insert</u> footers into the *Word* document.
5. <u>Save</u> your project to a floppy disk.
6. <u>Print</u> the *Word* document.
7. Staple the Transmittal Sheet on top of the report.
8. Compare by hand on the Transmittal Sheet the cash flows of the two corporations and explain which corporation appears to be a better investment from a cash flows perspective. Use the amounts in the worksheet on page 9.1 and the information about interpreting cash flows in Chapter 6 of your textbook.
9. <u>Copy</u> the worksheet.
10. <u>Print</u> the worksheet copy to show the formulas.
11. Staple the worksheet to the back of the Transmittal Sheet behind the report.

Project Nine Transmittal Sheet

Student Name: _____

Student Identification Number: _____

Class: _____

Date: _____

_____

_____

_____

_____

_____

_____

_____

_____

_____

_____

_____

_____

_____

_____

_____

_____

_____

_____

_____

_____

_____

_____

_____

_____

Notes:

Project Ten

Depreciation, Amortization & Depletion

Competencies

- Integrate *Microsoft® Excel* and *Microsoft® PowerPoint* to create a presentation that defines depreciation and demonstrates depreciation calculations.
- Define amortization and depletion, and demonstrate the calculations.

Project Data

Sheet 1. The formula in cell D16 is =(F9-F10)/F11
The formula in cell D25 is =C25/F11*2

	A	B	C	D	E	F	G
1							
2			STUDENT'S NAME CORPORATION				
3			DEPRECIATION SCHEDULES				
4			TODAY'S DATE				
5							
6		**DATA**					
7		Type of asset..				Computer	
8		Purchase year..				1999	
9		Cost of asset...				$60,000	
10		Salvage or residual value................................				$6,000	
11		Life of asset..				4	
12							
13		**CALCULATION--STRAIGHT LINE**					
14			Book Value	Depreciation	Accumulated	Book Value	
15		Year	Beg. of Year	Expense	Depreciation	End of Year	
16		1999	$60,000	$13,500	$13,500	$46,500	
17		2000	46,500				
18							
19							
20							
21							
22		**CALCULATION--DOUBLE DECLINING BALANCE**					
23			Book Value	Depreciation	Accumulated	Book Value	
24		Year	Beg. of Year	Expense	Depreciation	End of Year	
25		1999	$60,000	$30,000	$30,000	$30,000	
26		2000	30,000				
27							
28						6,000	
29							
30		**Project 10, Student's Name, Identification Number, Class Number, Today's Date**					

Outline of Slides 1 – 8:

Slide 1.   Title: Depreciation
              Sub-title: By
                          Student's Name

Slide 2.   Title: Topics For Discussion
              Bulleted list: Definition of depreciation
                          Data needed for depreciation calculations
                          Calculation of straight-line depreciation
                          Calculation of accelerated depreciation

Slide 3.   Title: Depreciation Defined
              Bulleted list: Depreciation is the process of allocating the cost of plant assets
                          over their estimated useful lives
                          Straight-line depreciation allocates equal portions of the cost
                          of each plant asset
                          Accelerated depreciation allocates a larger portion of the cost early
                          in each asset's life

Slide 4.   Title: Data Needed For Depreciation Calculations

                      [Insert Sheet 1, cells A1 – G12, into Slide 4.]

Slide 5.   Title: Straight-Line Depreciation

                      [Insert Sheet 1, cells A12 – G20, into Slide 5.]

Slide 6.   Title: Accelerated Depreciation

                      [Insert Sheet 1, cells A21 – G29, into Slide 6.]

Slide 7.   Title: Topics That Were Discussed
              Bulleted list: Definition of depreciation
                          Data needed for depreciation calculations
                          Calculation of straight-line depreciation
                          Calculation of accelerated depreciation

Slide 8.   Title: That's All, Folks!

The speech text (partially completed) is as follows:

1. Ladies and Gentlemen: My speech today is about depreciation at Student's Name Corporation.
2. The topics for discussion include… [Insert those listed on Slide 2.]

3. Depreciation is defined as... [Paraphrase the textbook definition.] Straight-line depreciation is defined as... Accelerated depreciation is defined as...
4. This slide shows the data needed for depreciation calculations. The data include...
5. This slide shows how straight-line depreciation is calculated at Student's Name Corporation. [Explain the table.]
6. This slide shows how double-declining balance depreciation is calculated at Student's Name Corporation. [Explain the table.]
7. In this presentation, I defined depreciation and showed how depreciation is calculated at Student's Name Corporation.
8. Thanks for listening! Are there any questions?

Required

> **Make sure that you complete the following steps in order. Refer to the procedures in the Appendix, which are alphabetized by underlined verb. Note the underlined verbs in the steps below.**

1. Open *Excel* and create the worksheet illustrated. Enter and format the numbers as shown in the data section. Enter a cell-based formula for each number in the calculation sections (including years). Apply a yellow fill color. The font should be bold and blue. Do not format the worksheets for printing at this time.
2. Open *PowerPoint* and create a *title slide*.
3. Apply a slide color scheme with a blue background and yellow and white font colors.
4. Insert a *bulleted list* format for slides 2, 3, and 7.
5. Insert a *title only* format for slides 4 – 6 and 8.
6. Apply *dissolve* as a slide transition effect for slides 2 – 7.
7. Apply *fly from bottom* as text preset animation for slides 2, 3, and 7.
8. Apply a *speech text* to slides 1 – 8. Complete the speech for slides 2 – 6. Use Chapter 10 in the textbook as a source of information.
9. Insert footers on to the notes pages.
10. Save your project to a floppy disk.
11. Print the slides as notes pages.
12. Attach the Transmittal Sheet to the front of the notes pages.
13. Explain (by hand on the Transmittal Sheet) the words *amortization* and *depletion*. Use hypothetical dollars to demonstrate how the amortization of an intangible asset, such as goodwill, is calculated. Use different dollars to demonstrate how the depletion of mineral rights is calculated.
14. Copy the worksheet.
15. Format the worksheet copy. Do not select guidelines.
16. Print the worksheet copy to show the formulas.
17. Attach the worksheet copy to the back of the notes pages.

Project Ten Transmittal Sheet

Student Name: _____

Student Identification Number: _____

Class: _____

Date: _____

_____

_____

_____

_____

_____

_____

_____

_____

_____

_____

_____

_____

_____

_____

_____

_____

_____

_____

_____

_____

_____

_____

_____

Notes:

Project Eleven

Analysis of Investing Activities

Competencies

- Integrate *Microsoft® Excel* and *Microsoft® Word* to create a report that uses financial statement information from two corporations to evaluate their investing activities.
- Explain the concept of operating leverage and why it should be considered when purchasing high-cost equipment.

Project Data

Sheet 1—Use cell-based formulas in cells C13 – F15 and cells C18 – F19

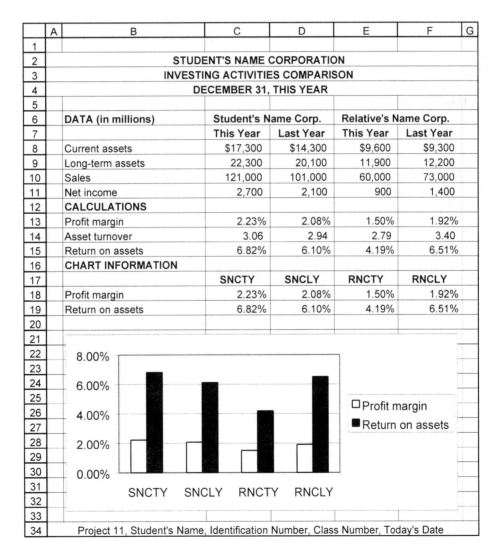

	A	B	C	D	E	F	G
1							
2		STUDENT'S NAME CORPORATION					
3		INVESTING ACTIVITIES COMPARISON					
4		DECEMBER 31, THIS YEAR					
5							
6		DATA (in millions)	Student's Name Corp.		Relative's Name Corp.		
7			This Year	Last Year	This Year	Last Year	
8		Current assets	$17,300	$14,300	$9,600	$9,300	
9		Long-term assets	22,300	20,100	11,900	12,200	
10		Sales	121,000	101,000	60,000	73,000	
11		Net income	2,700	2,100	900	1,400	
12		CALCULATIONS					
13		Profit margin	2.23%	2.08%	1.50%	1.92%	
14		Asset turnover	3.06	2.94	2.79	3.40	
15		Return on assets	6.82%	6.10%	4.19%	6.51%	
16		CHART INFORMATION					
17			SNCTY	SNCLY	RNCTY	RNCLY	
18		Profit margin	2.23%	2.08%	1.50%	1.92%	
19		Return on assets	6.82%	6.10%	4.19%	6.51%	
20							
21							
22							
...							
34		Project 11, Student's Name, Identification Number, Class Number, Today's Date					

Required

1. <u>Open</u> *Excel* and create a worksheet that looks like the example on page 11.1. <u>Merge and center</u> the text in rows 2, 3, 4, and 34. Use numbers in place of *This Year* and *Last Year* in Row 7. <u>Enter</u> and format the dollar amounts in the data section. <u>Enter</u> cell-based formulas and functions to calculate all amounts in cells C13 – F15 and cells C18 – F19. In Row 17, the letters SNCTY stand for the initials of *Student's Name Corporation* and *This Year*. The letters RNCTY stand for the initials of *Relative's Name Corporation* and *This Year*. Use the initials of your corporation and your relative's corporation, and numbers representing this year and last year.

2. <u>Format</u> each worksheet to include gridlines and row and column headings.

3. <u>Open</u> *Word* and create a double-spaced report from the information in Chapter 11 of your textbook. The report should have the title *Investing Activities Comparison by Student's Name* and a short introduction. <u>Insert</u> the *Excel* worksheet, cells A1 – G34, *as a picture* into the *Word* document under the introduction. Adjust the worksheet size so that it fits on the first page. The main body of the report should define each calculation and indicate which corporation is better as shown by that calculation. Cite specific amounts from the worksheet. The conclusion should include your observations about the worksheet calculations and which corporation is a better investment.

4. <u>Insert</u> footers into the *Word* document. The footers should include project number, student name, student identification, class number, and today's date.

5. <u>Save</u> your project to a floppy disk.

6. <u>Print</u> the *Word* document.

7. Staple the Transmittal Sheet on top of the report.

8. Explain by hand on the Transmittal Sheet the concept of operating leverage and why it should be considered when purchasing high-cost equipment.

9. <u>Copy</u> the worksheet.

10. <u>Print</u> the worksheet copy to show the formulas.

11. Staple the worksheet to the back of the Transmittal Sheet behind the report.

Project Eleven Transmittal Sheet

Student Name: _____

Student Identification Number: _____

Class: _____

Date: _____

_____
_____
_____
_____
_____
_____
_____
_____
_____
_____
_____
_____
_____
_____
_____
_____
_____
_____
_____
_____
_____
_____
_____

Notes:

Project Twelve

Operating Activities

Competencies

- Integrate *Microsoft® Excel* and *Microsoft® PowerPoint* to create a presentation that describes the purpose of income statements and their components.
- Discuss the special items that can affect the bottom line of an income statement.

Project Data

Sheet 1. This special format is required for the slide presentation.

	A	B	C	D	E
1					
2		STUDENT'S NAME CORPORATION			
3		INCOME STATEMENTS			
4		FOR YEARS ENDED DECEMBER 31,			
5					
6		(in thousands except per share data)	THIS YEAR	LAST YEAR	
7					
8		Sales and service revenue...................	$980,000	$920,000	
9		Cost of goods sold..............................	610,000	580,000	
10					
11		Gross profit.......................................	370,000	340,000	
12		Selling and administrative expenses...	250,000	230,000	
13					
14		Operating income..............................	120,000	110,000	
15					
16		(in thousands except per share data)	THIS YEAR	LAST YEAR	
17					
18		Operating income..............................	120,000	110,000	
19		Interest expense.................................	13,000	19,000	
20		Loss on sale of assets........................	1,500	1,000	
21					
22		Pretax income....................................	105,500	90,000	
23					
24		(in thousands except per share data)	THIS YEAR	LAST YEAR	
25					
26		Pretax income....................................	105,500	90,000	
27		Income taxes expense.........................	31,650	27,000	
28					
29		Net income..	$73,850	$63,000	
30					
31		Earnings per share.............................	$0.37	$0.32	
32					
33		Project 12, Student's Name, Class Number, Today's Date			

Outline of Slides 1 – 9:

Slide 1. Title: Purpose of Income Statements
  and Their Major Components
  Sub-title: By
  Student's Name

Slide 2. Title: Topics for Discussion
  Bulleted list: Purpose of income statements
  Heading component
  Operating activities component
  Other activities component
  "Who gets what" component

Slide 3. Title: Purpose of Income Statements
  Sub-title: To report the results of operating and other activities for fiscal
  periods on an accrual basis

Slide 4. Title: Heading Component

  [Insert Sheet 1, cells A1 – E7, into Slide 4.]

Slide 5. Title: Operating Activities Component

  [Insert Sheet 1, cells A5 – E15, into Slide 5.]

Slide 6. Title: Other Activities Component

  [Insert Sheet 1, cells A15 – E23, into Slide 6.]

Slide 7. Title: "Who Gets What" Component

  [Insert Sheet 1, cells A23 – E33, into Slide 7.]

Slide 8. Title: Topics Discussed
  Bulleted list: Purpose of income statements
  Heading component
  Operating activities component
  Financing and investing activities component
  "Who gets what" component

Slide 9. Title: That's All, Folks!

The speech text (partially completed) is as follows:

1. Ladies and Gentlemen: My speech today is about the income statements that are used at Student's Name Corporation.
2. My topics for discussion include the purpose of income statements and their components. The components are... [Name list on Slide 2.]
3. The purpose of the income statements used at Student's Name Corporation is...
4. The heading component contains the "who, what, and when" elements. The who is... The what shows that the report contains two... The when shows the two time periods affected by the report. The heading also shows how the amounts in the income statements are reported.
5. The operating activities component shows the income earned from the day-to-day activities of Student's Name Corporation. The top line shows... [Explain each line and include dollar amounts in your explanation.]
6. The other activities component shows pretax income earned after other items are added or subtracted from operating activities. At Student's Name Corporation... [Explain each line and include dollar amounts in your explanation.]
7. The "who gets what" component shows how the pretax income amounts are split between the government entities and the owners. The income taxes go to... The net income amounts are what's left for... [Explain the calculation of earnings per share.]
8. In this presentation, I discussed the purpose of the income statements used at Student's Name Corporation. I also discussed the purpose of each component.
9. Thanks for listening! Are there any questions?

Required

Make sure that you complete the following steps in order. Refer to the procedures in the Appendix, which are alphabetized by underlined verb. Note the underlined verbs in the steps below.

1. Open *Excel* and create the worksheet illustrated. Enter and format the numbers as shown in the data section. Use a yellow background and a blue font color. Do not set up the worksheet for printing.
2. Open *PowerPoint* and create a *title slide*.
3. Apply a slide color scheme with a blue background and yellow and white font colors.
4. Insert a *bulleted list* format for slides 2 and 8
5. Insert a *title* format for slide 3.
6. Insert a *title only* format for slides 4 – 7 and 9.
7. Apply *dissolve* as a slide transition effect for slides 2 – 9.
8. Apply *fly from bottom* as text preset animation for slides 2 and 8.
9. Apply a *speech text* to slides 1 – 9. Complete the speech for slides 2 – 7. Use Chapter 12 in the textbook as a source of information.
10. Insert footers on the notes pages.

11. <u>Save</u> your project to a floppy disk.
12. <u>Print</u> the slides as notes pages.
13. Attach the Transmittal Sheet to the front of the notes pages.
14. Discuss (by hand on the Transmittal Sheet) the special items that can affect the bottom line of an income statement. Use Chapters 5 and 12 in the textbook as a source of information.

Project Twelve Transmittal Sheet

Student Name: _____

Student Identification Number: _____

Class: _____

Date: _____

_____
_____
_____
_____
_____
_____
_____
_____
_____
_____
_____
_____
_____
_____
_____
_____
_____
_____
_____
_____
_____
_____
_____
_____

Notes:

Group Project Thirteen

Stock Portfolio

Competencies

- Integrate *Microsoft® Excel* and *Microsoft® Word* to create a report that evaluates the use of news articles, stock market prices, long-term trends, and financial statement analysis calculations for investing in stocks.
- Demonstrate how stocks are monitored and how stock transactions are recorded.

Project Data

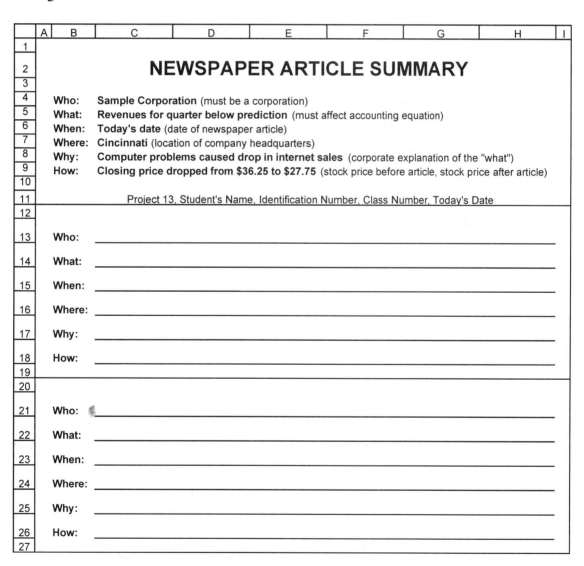

Sheet 1. The worksheet on the previous page shows the type of information that is summarized from newspaper articles. Room is given for the first two articles that you summarize.

Sheet 2. The worksheet on this page shows the quarterly market data taken from a hypothetical annual report. The chart made from the sample data shows that the time to buy may be during the 4th quarter of the year and the time to sell may be during the 1st quarter. Room is available for you to enter the stock prices from two actual annual reports.

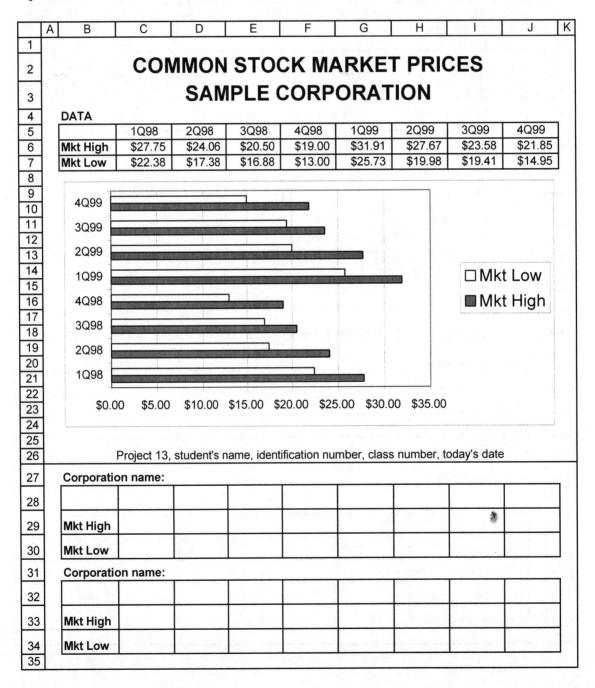

	A	B	C	D	E	F	G	H	I	J	K
1											
2		COMMON STOCK MARKET PRICES									
3		SAMPLE CORPORATION									
4		DATA									
5			1Q98	2Q98	3Q98	4Q98	1Q99	2Q99	3Q99	4Q99	
6		Mkt High	$27.75	$24.06	$20.50	$19.00	$31.91	$27.67	$23.58	$21.85	
7		Mkt Low	$22.38	$17.38	$16.88	$13.00	$25.73	$19.98	$19.41	$14.95	
8											
9–25		Chart (see figure)									
26		Project 13, student's name, identification number, class number, today's date									
27		Corporation name:									
28											
29		Mkt High									
30		Mkt Low									
31		Corporation name:									
32											
33		Mkt High									
34		Mkt Low									
35											

LONG-TERM TRENDS
SAMPLE CORPORATION

DATA   **Estimates**

Years ended	12/31/1997	12/31/1998	12/31/1999	12/31/2000	12/31/2001
Sales revenue	$870,000	$990,000	$1,100,000	$1,243,000	$1,430,000
Cost of sales	$514,000	$570,000	$590,000	$655,000	$727,000
Net Income	$44,000	$36,000	$31,000	$24,000	$18,000
Earnings per share	$1.20	$1.00	$0.90	$0.80	$0.70

CALCULATIONS   **Estimates**

	12/31/1997	12/31/1998	12/31/1999	12/31/2000	12/31/2001
Sales revenue	100.0%	113.8%	126.4%	142.9%	164.4%
Cost of sales	100.0%	110.9%	114.8%	127.4%	141.4%
Net Income	100.0%	81.8%	70.5%	54.5%	40.9%
Earnings per share	100.0%	83.3%	75.0%	66.7%	58.3%

Project 13, Student's Name, Identification Number, Class Number, Today's Date

Corporation name: **Estimates**

Years ended					
Sales revenue					
Cost of sales					
Net Income					
Earnings per share					

Corporation name: **Estimates**

Years ended					
Sales revenue					
Cost of sales					
Net Income					
Earnings per share					

Sheet 3. The worksheet on the previous page shows three years of data taken from a hypothetical annual report and two years of data that are estimated by you. The data are converted to percentages. The chart is based upon the percentages. Room is available for you to enter the long-term trends from two actual annual reports.

	A	B	C	D	E	F
1						
2		FINANCIAL STATEMENT			Annual Report Data	
3	DATA:	ANALYSIS				
4		Company name..	Sample Corp	Sample Corp		
5		Year ended...	12/31/1999	12/31/1999		
6		Dollars and shares (except per share data) in...........	Thousands	Thousands		
7		AR = accounts receivable...........................	72,000	72,000		
8		CA = current assets..................................	220,000	200,000		
9		CGS = cost of goods sold...........................	590,000	610,000		
10		CL = current liabilities...............................	115,000	115,000		
11		I = inventory..	102,000	82,000		
12		LTD = long-term debt...............................	150,000	150,000		
13		NI = net income (net earnings).....................	31,000	15,000		
14		OCF = operating cash flow..........................	49,000	49,000		
15		OI = operating income...............................	63,000	43,000		
16		OR = operating revenue (net sales)................	1,100,000	1,100,000		
17		SE = stockholders' equity...........................	200,000	180,000		
18		TA = total assets (current year)....................	465,000	445,000		
19		TAP = total assets (prior year).....................	397,000	387,000		
20	CALCULATIONS:					
21		Accounts receivable turnover =OR/AR..............	15.28	15.28		
22		Asset growth =(TA-TAP)/TAP.......................	17.13%	14.99%		
23		Asset turnover =OR/TA..............................	2.37	2.47		
24		Current ratio =CA/CL................................	1.91	1.74		
25		Debt to assets ratio =LTD/TA.......................	32.26%	33.71%		
26		Debt to equity ratio =LTD/SE.......................	75.00%	83.33%		
27		Financial leverage =TA/SE..........................	2.33	2.47		
28		Gross profit margin =(OR-CGS)/OR.................	46.36%	44.55%		
29		Inventory turnover =CGS/ I..........................	5.78	7.44		
30		Operating cash flow to total assets ratio =OCF/TA......	10.54%	11.01%		
31		Operating income margin =OI/OR...................	5.73%	3.91%		
32		Profit margin =NI/OR.................................	2.82%	1.36%		
33		Return on assets =NI/TA.............................	6.67%	3.37%		
34		Return on equity =NI/SE.............................	15.50%	8.33%		
35		Working capital =CA-CL.............................	$105,000	$85,000		
36						
37		Project 13, Student Name, Identification Number, Class Number, Today's Date				

Sheet 4. The above worksheet shows data taken from the most current year of a hypothetical annual report. The calculations are made using cell-based formulas. Room is available for you to enter data and calculations from two actual annual reports.

STOCK MONITORING WORKSHEET

NAME OF CORPORATION:

	Trans.	Ticker	No. of	Purchase Price		Market Price		Unrealized	Selling Price		Realized
	Date	Symbol	Shares	Per Share	Total	Per Share	Total	Gain (loss)	Per Share	Total	Gain (loss)
7											
8											
9											
10											
11											
12											
13											
14											
15											
16											

NAME OF CORPORATION:

	Trans.	Ticker	No. of	Purchase Price		Market Price		Unrealized	Selling Price		Realized
	Date	Symbol	Shares	Per Share	Total	Per Share	Total	Gain (loss)	Per Share	Total	Gain (loss)
21											
22											
23											
24											
25											
26											
27											
28											
29											
30											

Project 13, Student Name, Identification Number, Class Number, Today's Date

Name of corporation: SAMPLE CORP.

	Trans.	Ticker	No. of	Purchase Price		Market Price		Unrealized	Selling Price		Realized
	Date	Symbol	Shares	Per Share	Total	Per Share	Total	Gain (loss)	Per Share	Total	Gain (loss)
37	09/15/1999	SMPL	900	32.83	29,547						
38	10/22/1999	SMPL	900			32.25	29,025	(522)			
39	11/24/1999	SMPL	900						33.17	29,853	306

Sheet 5. The above worksheet shows the purchase price, market price, and sales price of a hypothetical stock in rows 37 – 39. You can record in rows 15 – 38 the purchase, price changes, and sale of two stocks that are actually traded. You should have the annual reports of the two corporations before you purchase the stock.

	A	B	C	D	E	F	G	H
1		USING A MODIFIED JOURNAL						
2	Trans.	Account Name And	Financial Statement Effects				Enter Amount As	
3	Date	Ticker Symbol	A =	L +	E +	NI	Debit	Credit
4	OPEN ACCOUNT AT BROKERAGE							
5		Cash	+				60,000	
6		Capital			+			60,000
7	PURCHASE COMMON STOCK							
8		Securities--trading [ ]						
9		Securities--trading [ ]						
10		Cash						
11	RECEIVE CASH DIVIDENDS							
12		Cash						
13		Dividend revenue [ ]						
14		Dividend revenue [ ]						
15	SELL COMMON STOCK							
16		Cash						
17		Securities--trading [ ]						
18		Securities--trading [ ]						
19		Gain (Loss) on securities						
20								
21						TOTALS		
22								
23	Project 13, Student's Name, Identification Number, Class Number, Today's Date							

Sheet 6L. You can record your actual stock transactions in the modified journal (shown above) using debit and credit entries. This is a modification of the journal format shown in the textbook.

Sheet 6R. You can record the same stock transactions in the spreadsheet (shown on the next page) as increases or decreases to the balance sheet or income statement. This is a modification of the spreadsheet format shown in the textbook.

	I	J	K	L	M	N	O
1	USING A SPREADSHEET						
2	BALANCE SHEET				INCOME STATEMENT		
3	Cash +	Securities	= Liab.	+ Equity	+ Div. Rev.	+ Gains	- Losses
4							
5	60,000						
6				60,000			
7							
8							
9							
10							
11							
12							
13							
14							
15							
16							
17							
18							
19							
20							
21							
22							
23							

Required

> **Make sure that you complete the following steps in order. Refer to the procedures in the Appendix, which are alphabetized by underlined verb. Note the underlined verbs in the steps below.**

A. At the beginning of the semester or quarter, request annual reports from at least two mid-sized manufacturing or merchandising corporations (Your instructor may provide these). The corporations must be listed under the New York Stock Exchange Composite Transactions, NASDAQ National Market Issues, or American Stock

Exchange Composite Transactions in the *Wall Street Journal*. Record the annual report information in the worksheets shown on pages 13.2 – 13.4 of this project.

B. Summarize (at least once per week) newspaper articles about the two corporations discussed in your annual reports on the worksheet shown on page 13.1 of this project. Summarize news of other public corporations if you cannot find news on your two companies.

C. Invest no more than $60,000 in the two corporations discussed by your annual reports. Invest approximately $40,000 in the corporation with the best potential. Invest approximately $20,000 in the other corporation. Add 1% commission per share to each stock purchase. Record the stock purchases in the worksheets shown on pages 13.5 – 13.7.

D. Monitor the stocks in your portfolio at least once per week. Record the market per share and total prices and unrealized gain (loss) in the worksheet shown on page 13.5.

E. Check the news as to when dividends are paid. Record the cash dividends received from your corporations (if any) in the worksheet shown on pages 13.6 – 13.7.

F. Sell the stocks near the end of the semester or quarter. Use selling prices that equal the closing prices on the sale date less 1% commission. Record the selling per share and total prices and the realized gain (loss) in the worksheets on pages 13.5 – 13.7.

G. Open an Excel workbook and create worksheets similar to those shown on pages 13.1 – 13.7. Replace the sample company data with actual data. Use cell-based formulas for all calculations.

H. Create a Word document along with other class members assigned to your group. The cover page should show the title *Group Project 13: Stock Portfolio Report*, today's date, class number, companies, and names of students assigned to the group. The report should evaluate two analysis tools for short-term investing and two analysis tools for long-term investing. *Explain how the tools can be used by your group members to make common stock purchase decisions today.* Insert *Excel* data and charts collected by each student in the group into the *Word* document as illustrations. The report should contain an introduction (2 – 3 sentences), main section with references to inserted worksheet illustrations and charts, and conclusion. The report should use analysis tools from the following list:

1. Reports on news articles (include best example from each group member)
2. Charts showing common stock market prices (best from each group member)
3. Charts showing long-term trends for corporations (best from each group member)
4. Key financial statement analysis calculations (worksheet from each member)

I. Attach to the back of the group report the following *Excel* worksheets from each group member:

1. A stock monitoring worksheet for two companies similar to the one on page 13.5
2. A journal and spreadsheet (combined on one worksheet in landscape format) similar to the worksheet illustrated on pages 13.6 and 13.7

A Transmittal Sheet is not required with this project.